The Universe

Written by Gail Saunders-Smith

STECK-VAUGHN
COMPANY

A Division of Harcourt Brace & Company

www.steck-vaughn.com

T 42149

Contents

Chapter 1

The Universe and Us

When you look at the night sky, you probably see the moon and the stars. You might even see a shooting star. But did you know that the universe has billions more things that you can't see?

The universe is all of space and everything in it. It is so big that we have trouble just thinking about its size. Some of the objects in the universe are as big as our sun. Some of them are as tiny as a speck of dust. Some of the objects are beautiful. Some of them are weird. All of them are interesting.

The universe has billions of stars. Some stars have planets spinning around them. The star and its planets are called a **solar system**.

Our solar system's star is called the sun. Nine planets **orbit**, or travel around, it. The four planets closest to the sun are hard and rocky. The next four planets are huge and gassy. The ninth planet is so far away from the sun that some scientists aren't even sure it is a planet!

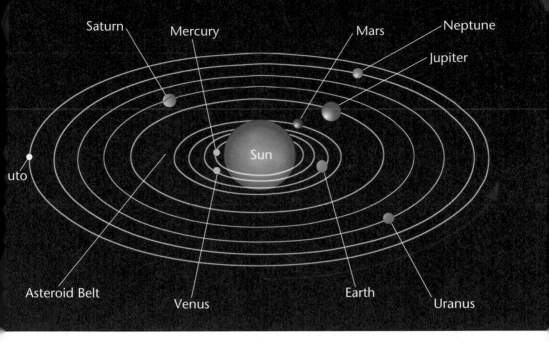

The planets and asteroids orbit the sun.

Long ago people studied the sky at night. Sometimes they were frightened by flashes of light or other strange things they saw in the sky. But people always asked questions about what they saw. Inventions like the telescope helped people find out more about the universe.

People still look up at the twinkling darkness and wonder. Rockets and satellites now help us explore the universe. What do you look for in the night sky? What do you wonder about?

◀ This model shows how our solar system's planets differ in size.

Chapter 2

The Sun

The sun is the center of our solar system. It is hot and bright now, but it was not always that way. The sun began as a huge cloud of dust and gases. The dust and gases were pulled together. They became tightly packed, and the cloud grew hotter and hotter. Finally the cloud was hot enough to shine.

The center of the sun is really hot—about 29 million° F (16 million° C). The outside of the sun is not as hot as the center. If you look at the sun through a special telescope, you can see dark patches. These are called sun spots. Sun spots are cooler than the area around them.

Sun spots show up as dark spots on the sun's surface.

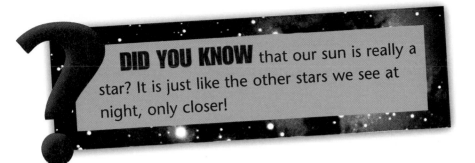

The sun is the largest object in our solar system. It is almost as big as everything else in our solar system put together. In fact, it would take more than a *million* Earths to equal the size of the sun! It doesn't look that big, does it? That's because it is very far away from us—about 90 million miles (145 million kilometers) away!

The sun is almost 5 billion years old. Scientists think it will stay the way it is for another 4½ billion years. Then it will change. At first it will get bigger and much brighter. Then it will shrink and slowly grow dim. All the other parts of our solar system will be left in cold darkness.

The sun is very far away, but it gives off a tremendous amount of light. You should never look straight at it. It is too bright. It is so bright that you could be blinded.

An eclipse is a darkening of something. A **solar eclipse** is a darkening of the sun. The sun doesn't really stop giving off light. What happens is that the moon comes between Earth and the sun. The moon blocks the sun's light.

People of long ago became very frightened during eclipses. They believed that angry sky gods were taking away light and warmth to punish them.

Here on Earth, the darkness during a solar eclipse can make noon seem like early evening. The darkness doesn't last very long, though. The longest solar eclipses last about 7½ minutes. Most last about 3 minutes.

During a solar eclipse, powerful telescopes let us see parts of the sun we usually cannot. For example, we can see the **corona** and solar flares. The corona is the sun's top layer of gas. It looks like a halo spreading out from the sun. Solar flares are huge jets of hot gas that shoot up from the sun's surface.

A model of a solar eclipse. The sun is behind the moon. ▶

Moon

Earth

Chapter 3

The moon is our nearest space neighbor, but it is still about 240,000 miles (390,000 kilometers) from Earth. And it is smaller than our planet. It would take 4 moons to equal the size of Earth. Many scientists think that the moon was created when a space object hit Earth. Pieces of the object and Earth then came together to form the moon.

The moon is very hot in some places and very cold in others. Places hit by the sun reach a temperature of 261° F (127° C). Places in the shade dip to –279° F (–173° C).

The outside of the moon has flat, dark areas and high areas that show up more brightly. The dark places are called seas. A sea on the moon isn't made of water. It is made of dust.

The moon also has big dents in it. These dents are called **craters**. They were made when large pieces of other space objects slammed into the surface of the moon.

The same part of the moon is always turned toward Earth.

The moon's gravity is not nearly as strong as Earth's. The weaker pull makes a person weigh only ⅙ as much as the person does on Earth. That means a child who weighs 60 pounds (27 kilograms) on Earth weighs only 10 pounds (4½ kilograms) on the moon. With less gravity, you can bounce really high. Think about the great jump shots you could make if you played basketball on the moon!

As nights go by, the moon seems to get larger, then smaller. The moon's size doesn't really change, though. What changes is the amount of sunlight that we see reflected off the moon. These changes in sunlight create the phases of the moon.

The phases of the moon from one new moon to the next

When we see no moon, it is because no sunlight is being reflected off it. This phase is called a new moon. Each night after that, we see more of the sun's light reflecting off the moon. Then the whole surface of the moon shines with the sun's light. We call that phase a full moon. After a full moon, we begin to see less sunlight reflecting off the moon. Then the moon is all dark again. The full cycle from new moon to new moon takes about 29 days.

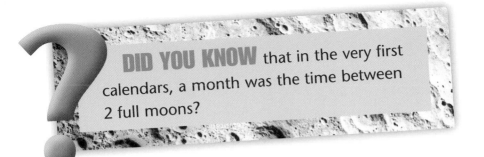

DID YOU KNOW that in the very first calendars, a month was the time between 2 full moons?

Astronauts first walked on the moon in 1969. While there, the astronauts did experiments, left a United States flag, and even played golf. Since that first trip, astronauts have brought back about 840 pounds (381 kilograms) of moon rocks and moon dirt for scientists to study. Yes, rocks and dirt! Not a bit of cheese!

An astronaut on the moon in 1971

Chapter 4

Mercury is the closest planet to the sun. On a clear night, Mercury is one of the planets that we can see from Earth without a telescope.

Mercury orbits the sun much faster than Earth does. It goes around the sun in only 88 days. You know that it takes Earth 365 days to orbit the sun. We call that 365 days a year. A year on Mercury, then, is only 88 days long.

Mercury's orbit is strange. Mercury swings close to one side of the sun and swings twice as far out on the other side. The side of Mercury close to the sun is really hot, about 810° F (430° C). The other side is super cold.

The surface of Mercury is made of rough, dark rock. It looks a lot like the surface of our moon. Mercury has few gases around it, so we say it has little **atmosphere**.

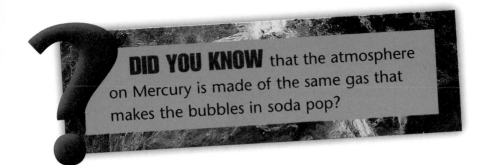

Mercury **rotates**, or spins, much more slowly than Earth does. On Earth we say that 1 complete spin is a day. Because of Mercury's slow spin, a day there is as long as 176 Earth days!

Mercury's surface is covered with craters.

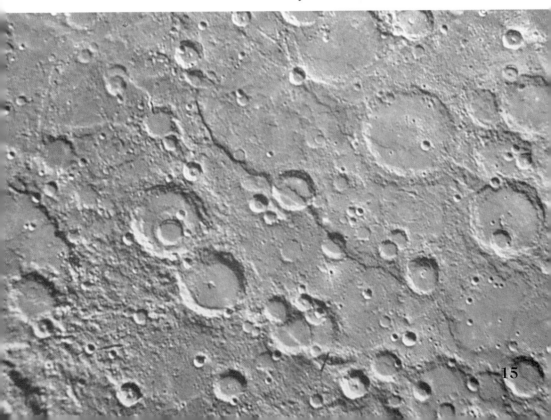

Venus is the second planet from the sun. Of all the planets, Venus is closest in size to Earth. It has been called the Morning Star and the Evening Star because it looks like a pretty white spot in the morning sky and night sky. Venus looks white to us because the sun's light reflects off the thick cloud layer around the planet.

The Evening Star is really the planet Venus.

The thick cloud layer of Venus, seen from space

Radar telescopes have allowed many scientists on Earth to look through the thick cloud cover on Venus. They can see volcanoes and craters and large, flat areas. If you could stand on Venus and look up, the sky would appear reddish because the air is so thick with gases.

Venus gets about twice as hot as a kitchen oven can get. It is hotter than Mercury, even though it is farther from the sun than Mercury. Why? The heat from the sun gets trapped under the thick atmosphere and cannot get out. So it gets really, really hot.

One day on Venus lasts 243 Earth days. Can you imagine? If you could live on Venus, each school day would be about 81 Earth days long!

Chapter 5

Home, Sweet Home

From space, Earth looks like a blue and white ball in a vast black sky. It is a little flat at each **pole**. It bulges around the middle. You know that a long time ago, people thought Earth was flat. Do you know why they thought that? When they looked at the horizon, they thought it was the edge of Earth.

As Earth spins, one side faces the sun. This side is having daytime. The other side faces away from the sun, so it is dark. This side is having nighttime. A complete spin of Earth takes 23 hours, 56 minutes, and 4 seconds. We often round this time to 24 hours, and we call it a day.

The average temperature on Earth is 59° F (15° C). The hottest temperature ever recorded is 136° F (58° C). The lowest is −129° F (−90° C).

In this photograph of Earth, you can see ▶
North America and South America.

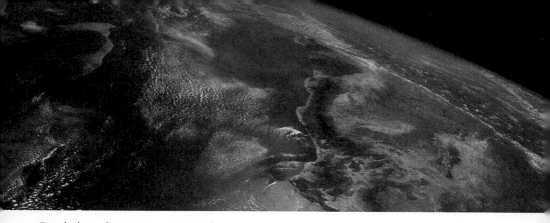

Earth has far more water than land.

Earth is the only place we know of so far that has life. Some of the life forms are plants, and some are animals. We are one of the animal life forms. Earth is the only planet that has enough oxygen to allow living things to stay alive.

The surface of Earth is mainly water. Most of the water is found in the oceans. Some is found in rivers, lakes, and other bodies of fresh water.

Land makes up only about ⅓ of Earth's surface. The largest bodies of land are the continents. The continents have different kinds of surfaces. Some are low and have lots of plant life. Other surfaces are high and rocky. Many of these surfaces have almost no plant life. Africa and South America have hot, steamy forests. Antarctica is buried under ice and snow.

Chapter 6

Mars and Jupiter

In many ways Mars is the planet most like Earth. It has canyons, volcanoes, and desert areas. Mars also seems to have seasons like we do. Scientists have discovered that huge ice caps form at its north and south poles at different times of the Martian year. Then they melt.

We can see Mars without a telescope. Because its surface and sky look reddish, Mars is often called the Red Planet. The color comes from the large amount of iron on the planet.

Mars is the color of fire, but it is really a cold planet.

The surface of Mars is dusty and rocky and has many craters. It also has straight gorges. Some people once thought that smart creatures from Mars dug the gorges and used them as waterways. People called the smart creatures Martians. But scientists have discovered that the gorges were made naturally, not by Martians.

Jupiter is the largest planet in our solar system. It may also be the most unusual. Jupiter is made of the same gas as the sun, but it is too small to be a star. It is so huge that more than 1000 Earths could fit inside it. Jupiter spins so fast that one day is only 10 Earth hours long.

Jupiter has bands of color that swirl and move around its middle. These are clouds that are pulled into wide strips of color by the planet's fast rotation.

Jupiter has a Great Red Spot that can be seen with a telescope from Earth. The Great Red Spot is actually a monstrous storm. Sometimes it is as large as Earth and sometimes even larger.

Jupiter is a ball of gas.

Jupiter has at least 16 moons. One of the moons, Io, has 9 volcanoes that spew molten, poisonous sulfur about 60 miles (97 kilometers) straight up. Io has more volcanoes than any other place in the solar system. Another moon, Europa, is the smoothest place in our solar system. Europa has no craters and no mountains. It is only cracked sheets of ice.

DID YOU KNOW that Jupiter has the worst weather in the galaxy? The clouds are full of bad storms. The winds there are like hurricane winds on Earth.

The asteroid belt contains thousands of asteroids.

Between Mars and Jupiter floats a ring of small space objects. This ring is called the **asteroid** belt. An asteroid is a chunk of rock. Some scientists think that the asteroids in the asteroid belt were once a planet between Jupiter and Mars. They think the planet broke apart.

Chapter 7

Saturn and Uranus

Saturn is the second-largest planet. Days on Saturn are only 10½ Earth hours long. But years are very long. One year on Saturn lasts for 29½ Earth years.

The most striking thing about Saturn is its 7 rings. They orbit the middle of the planet in a thin, flat sheet. The rings extend about 45,000 miles (72,000 kilometers) out into space.

Saturn's rings always tilt in the same direction as the planet.

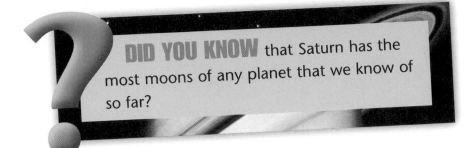

DID YOU KNOW that Saturn has the most moons of any planet that we know of so far?

Some scientists think the rings are made of moons that were blasted apart by other space objects. Some rings have water and might be made of chunks of ice. Some rings have particles of dust.

Saturn has 18 moons. Most of them are very small. They move around the planet and help keep the rings in place. The largest moon, Titan, has an atmosphere.

Saturn's rings are made of many smaller rings.

Uranus is a strange place. Uranus has 15 moons and 10 rings. It looks blue-green when viewed through a telescope.

Uranus tilts so much that it looks like it is spinning from top to bottom instead of around the sides. Scientists think it is tilted because something slammed into it a long time ago and knocked it on its side.

The rings around Uranus are small and very thin. Some are made of chunks of ice, some are made of dust, and some are made of both. Small moons keep Uranus's rings separated. One of the moons is called Miranda. Miranda is made of smeared rock that looks like peanut butter spread on bread. A huge cliff sticks out from Miranda, and a giant check mark can be seen on the surface.

A gas in its atmosphere gives Uranus its blue-green color.

Chapter 8

Neptune and Pluto

Seen through a telescope here on Earth, Neptune is just a tiny blue spot. Yet it would take 60 Earths to equal the size of Neptune.

Neptune has to go a long way to get around the sun. It takes 165 Earth years. That means a Neptune year has 60,225 Earth days!

Neptune has 8 moons and 5 rings. The largest of Neptune's moons is called Triton. This large moon has active volcanoes. These volcanoes are not like the ones on Earth. They erupt ice instead of lava. The ice eruptions can spray across Triton for 100 miles.

Neptune can only be seen with a telescope.

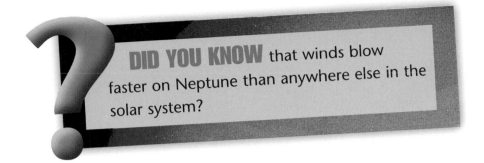

Pluto is the farthest object from the sun in our solar system. It is the only planet that has not been studied by a spacecraft. Some scientists think that Pluto isn't even a real planet. Some think it may be a moon that was pulled away from Neptune.

It takes Pluto 249 Earth years to orbit the sun. During 20 of those years, Pluto cuts in front of Neptune. This change in orbit makes Pluto closer to the sun than Neptune is for a while.

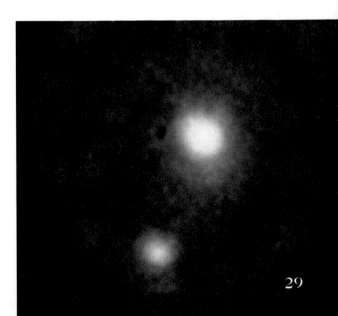

Pluto and its moon, Charon.

Chapter 9
Twinkle, Twinkle, Little Stars

On a clear night, we can see about 2000 stars with just our eyes. In all, there are more stars than anyone could ever count, no matter how long that person counted.

Each of the stars we see in the night sky is a burning, fiery ball just like the sun at the center of our solar system. Some stars are smaller than the sun, and some are larger. Some are older, and some are younger. Some may have planets around them like ours does. The star nearest

Earth is Proxima Centuri. It is about 25 trillion miles (40 trillion kilometers) away from us.

Long ago, people thought groups of stars formed pictures. Today these groups of stars are called **constellations**. Some people saw a hunter pulling back a bow to shoot an arrow. They named him Orion. Some people saw twin boys and called them Gemini.

A group of stars that looked like a little bear was named Ursa Minor. A pattern that looked like a big bear was named Ursa Major. Parts of Ursa Minor and Ursa Major are also known as the Little Dipper and the Big Dipper. The constellation for the dragon was named Draco. The lion was named Leo.

Although they seem to, stars do not move across the sky at night. Because Earth rotates, the stars just seem to move. Constellations help sailors find their way around the oceans by letting them know which way is north, south, east, or west.

◀ Stars shine all the time, but we can only see them on a clear, dark night.

The star maps below show some well-known constellations.

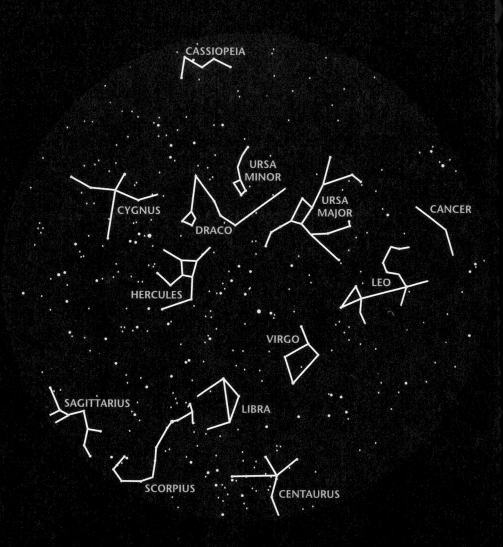

Summer
Constellations

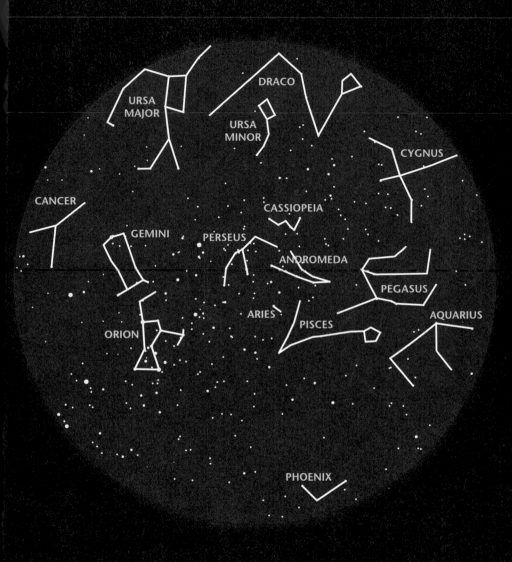

DRACO

URSA MAJOR

URSA MINOR

CYGNUS

CANCER

CASSIOPEIA

GEMINI

PERSEUS

ANDROMEDA

ARIES

PEGASUS

ORION

PISCES

AQUARIUS

PHOENIX

Winter Constellations

Chapter 10

Meteors, Comets, and Galaxies

If you have ever studied the night sky, you may have seen a bright streak of light. People call this a falling star or a shooting star. It's really a **meteor**.

A meteor starts out as a **meteoroid**, a chunk of rock or metal in outer space. When the meteoroid enters Earth's atmosphere, it burns and glows. Then it is called a meteor. If anything of the meteor is left to hit Earth's surface, it is then called a **meteorite**.

The largest meteorite that we know of fell in Africa. It weighed about 132,000 pounds (60,000 kilograms). That's more than 10 elephants weigh! Scientists have discovered 80 meteorite craters on Earth. Some scientists think a giant meteorite crashed into Earth long ago and led to the death of the dinosaurs.

Comet Hale-Bopp

A **comet** is a huge bunch of dust and ice. The best time to see one is at sunrise or sunset. The head of a comet can be 50 miles (81 kilometers) across or even larger. The tail of a comet can be thousands or millions of miles long! We can't see the tail of a comet until the comet gets close to the sun. The tail gets longer as the comet gets closer to the sun.

As of 1995, scientists had discovered more than 800 comets. About 184 comets come around about every 200 years. Halley's Comet comes around once every 76 years. We last saw it in 1986.

Comet Hale-Bopp was discovered in 1995. It was seen by two men in two different places. They reported it at the same time, so the comet was named for both of them.

The universe has huge groups of stars. Each group is called a **galaxy**. Our galaxy is the Milky Way Galaxy. The Milky Way is only one galaxy out of billions. Scientists think it is made up of 100,000 million stars—that's 100 trillion stars. The galaxy nearest to ours is called the Andromeda Galaxy. It would take four Milky Ways to equal the size of Andromeda.

Some people think that in all the trillions of stars, there may be a solar system like ours—a solar system with a planet that has life. Could there be someone or something else out there on another planet in another galaxy? What do you think?

The Andromeda Galaxy ▶

37

Glossary

asteroid a small, rocky space body

atmosphere the layer of gases around a
planet

comet a clump of dust and ice that orbits
the sun

constellation a group of stars that forms a
picture

corona the top layer of gas that spreads
out from the sun

crater a hole made by a space object
smashing into the surface of a planet or
a moon

galaxy a group of stars held together by
gravity

meteor a meteoroid that enters Earth's
atmosphere (also called a shooting star)

meteorite a piece of a meteor that fell to
Earth

meteoroid a chunk of rock or metal in space

orbit to circle an object, such as the sun; the curved path made by a planet or moon

pole the top or bottom of a planet

rotate to spin

solar eclipse the darkening of the sun when the moon blocks its light

solar system a star, such as the sun, and all the bodies that orbit it

Index